FASTBACK® Science Fiction

Sinking Ship

DAVE SMEDS

GLOBE FEARON
Pearson Learning Group

FASTBACK® SCIENCE FICTION BOOKS

The Champion	In the Zone
Dateline: I.P.S.	Just in Case
Eden's Daughters	**Sinking Ship**
The Flavorist	The Spotter
Hennesy's Test	Vital Force

Cover David Emite Photos/Stone/Getty Images. All photography © Pearson Education, Inc. (PEI) unless specifically noted.

Copyright © 2004 by Pearson Education, Inc., publishing as Globe Fearon®, an imprint of Pearson Learning Group, 299 Jefferson Road, Parsippany, NJ 07054. All rights reserved. No part of this book may be reproduced or transmitted in any form or by any means, electronic or mechanical, including photocopying, recording, or by any information storage and retrieval system, without permission in writing from the publisher. For information regarding permission(s), write to Rights and Permissions Department.

Globe Fearon® and Fastback® are registered trademarks of Globe Fearon, Inc.

ISBN 0-13-024579-8
Printed in the United States of America
1 2 3 4 5 6 7 8 9 10   07 06 05 04 03

1-800-321-3106
www.pearsonlearning.com

The *Valiant* was deep inside Helvan space when the attack came. Alan heard the alarms and sprinted across the sick bay. Within eight seconds he had strapped himself into an examining couch. Three seconds later the *Valiant* was struck.

The room jumped. The shock wave flung Alan upward against the straps and then back down into the couch. It knocked the wind out of him. The ship groaned. They'd been hit. Badly.

The lights went out.

Alan gasped, struggling to fill his lungs. The sick-bay batteries kicked in. Power was restored to the med sensors and to some of the lights. The room was cast in a dim glow. The alarm had switched off.

What if I'm the only one left? Alan thought. He tried to quiet the screaming in his nerves and brain. Then the intercom blared to life.

"Status reports! All stations, report!"

It was Chief Petty Officer Fred Westin. That shouldn't be. Why was an enlisted man taking charge? What had happened to the commander? Alan jabbed a finger at the intercom button.

"Sick bay, minor damage," Alan reported. He could hear other departments checking in. The sounds of the familiar voices comforted him.

The greenhouse and the galley were intact. The rec lounge had a hole in it.

"I can't raise the bridge," Fred was shouting. "Engineering, what's happening?"

Alan heard a beep coming from the life-support monitor. A yellow light flashed overhead.

The room was losing oxygen. Alan flipped several switches to seal off the sick bay. The monitor stopped making noise. Good. That meant the leak was outside the medical section. If the ship were hit again, that could easily change.

"The bridge is gone!" The speaker sounded young. "Commander Feldon is dead."

"Engineering here," said a pained voice. "Severe damage . . ."

Alan reached for his space suit. He was halfway into it when Nurse Sheila Tamm stepped out of the air lock. They listened in shock to the report from engineering. From that station, the speaker had a view of the entire ship.

"Bridge wiped out. Nothing but burned girders and sparks. Severe damage to living quarters. Gunnery level intact . . ." The words became more labored. Then they stopped altogether.

Alan's heart was pounding. If the gunnery level weren't damaged, they could still shoot back. Alan and Sheila huddled together, waiting for another impact. Instead, a joyous yell jumped from the intercom.

"I got 'em! I nailed 'em!" Alan recognized the accent. It was Zack Emmett, the gunner.

Alan and Sheila hugged each other. The battle was over. For the moment, at least, they were safe.

The *Valiant* was a mess. As Alan and the nurses treated injured crew members, the voices over the intercom told what had happened.

Enemy fire had split open the *Valiant*'s hull. Anyone exposed to the vacuum of space had died right away. Those who survived had been in chambers that held oxygen long enough for them to climb into suits.

The bridge was totally destroyed. All communications and most navigational systems were gone. Also taken were the lives of every commanding officer.

Alan had just put the third injured crew member on his table when the gravity went out. His feet left the floor. He had to grab his scissors from the air. The injured man yelled, shocked by the sudden change. Alan strapped his patient down. Then he connected himself to the table with a tether. He continued working. Just as he had finished, two men pulled the chief engineer into the room.

Alan dropped what he was doing and helped pull the chief out of his space suit. The man was bleeding from the abdomen and mouth. "Sheila!" Alan barked. "We've got major surgery here!"

Sheila rushed forward, leaving the minor injuries to Michael, the other nurse. Within seconds they had the chief strapped into the med couch. He was moaning, his breath coming in ragged wheezes.

"Easy, Ben," Alan said. "We'll get you fixed right up."

Alan turned on the med sensor. The readout appeared on the large screen to his right. He saw an outline of Ben's body, coded in bright colors. He adjusted the image until the blood vessels stood out in red and blue. Ben's colon, right lung, and right kidney were damaged. Alan quickly checked the blood pressure and the white blood-cell count. He took extra time examining the broken ribs. Breaks were bad news in a non-gravity environment. Weightlessness didn't provide the stress needed to make bones knit together properly.

"My poor babies," Ben mumbled.

Alan shot a puzzled look at the two midshipmen who had brought Ben in. "He means the engines," one of them explained.

Alan hesitated. "How bad is it?"

The midshipman didn't answer. He merely shook his head in worry.

Alan tried to keep his eyes open. He was exhausted. It had been 30 hours since the attack. He had not slept. Ben's surgery was only one of many urgent demands.

The other crew members had not fared much better. Anyone who was able to was struggling to repair the ship. They had to patch holes and save as much air as possible. There wasn't enough air in the tanks to refill the whole ship. Some equipment was too fragile to leave exposed to a total vacuum. The crew had to save the plants in the greenhouse. They had to get power to the heating units. By the time everyone gathered to talk about long-term problems, they were worn out.

Alan let his body relax as much as he could. He knew that lack of gravity would keep him from falling down. He wished he could sleep where he was standing. There were too many people pressing into the small room. Alan kept being jostled.

At last all of the crew had arrived. Acting Commander Fred Westin addressed them from the middle of the room.

"I would like to thank everyone for their hard work these many hours," he said. Fred was ill at ease with his new role as commander. "First the good news. Over half the ship is now airtight. Most of those sections have power and some degree of climate control. For now, you are advised to remain in your suits when you're working in areas near the hull. Our food supplies are intact. There's enough for almost a year considering the number of mouths we have to feed." Fred glanced sadly around the room. Only 25 out of a crew of 55 had survived. "And finally, it seems we were attacked by only one ship. As far as we can tell, we destroyed it."

Fred cleared his throat. "Now, the bad news," he continued. "As you know, we're in Helvan territory. We've lost every officer except me and the chief engineer. He'll be bedridden for some time. We have no hope of rescue by friendly forces. We can send up a distress signal and hope that the Helvans will take the trouble to make us prisoners. If that happens, we'll be locked up until the war is over. We could also try to get back home."

"What about the engines?" a bosun's mate asked.

Fred sighed. "Three of them are damaged beyond repair. The fourth has only minor damage, but for some reason it won't power up. All circuits are dead. Now that the ship is relatively stable, we can take a closer look at that fourth engine. I'm hoping for the best. However, the first thing we all need is rest. That's an *order!* Once we're alert, we'll be much more capable of doing what we have to do."

After news like that, Alan thought, getting to sleep would be difficult.

Alan awoke to soft purring sounds. They came from the air vents and from the nurses snoring on the other side of the room. The medical staff had bunked down in a small room near the main sick bay. The clock on the wall told Alan he was only halfway through his sleep period. But Alan sensed something different about the ship.

He unbuckled the restraining strap and pushed himself off the bed. Then he settled back onto the mattress. Suddenly he knew what had awakened him.

It was a slight change, perhaps a twentieth of a G. But compared to no gravity at all, Alan was surprised he hadn't noticed it sooner. He glanced at Sheila and Michael and slipped from the room without waking them.

One deck down from sick bay, Alan entered the weather-control center.

There he found engineers Kay and Terry crouched around a pile of charred consoles. They were picking up a bank of relays. Everything had settled to the floor under the return of gravity. Grease, sweat, and weariness marked Kay's and Terry's faces.

"Hello, Alan," said Terry. She seemed barely able to make the effort to speak. Kay nodded as she checked the gravity indicators. She wiped a bit of grime from her nose and said, "It's not much, but it's the best I can do. I can't put any more stress on the ship until we strengthen the hull."

"Climate control is next," Terry promised.

It was almost tropical, but Alan ignored the heat. "Aren't you two supposed to be sleeping?" he asked.

"We did sleep. We will sleep," Kay said. "This is more important."

Alan decided not to press the issue. He knew these two well. They often spent 18 hours straight in their shop and barely came out to eat. Their response to stress was to bury themselves in their work. In many ways these two were the *Valiant*'s only hope.

Spacedrive engines were not their specialty. Yet Terry and Kay were wizards at everything mechanical and electrical. If anyone could get the ship moving, it was these two.

"All right. But please don't overdo it," Alan said. "You'll want to be as alert as you can when we pull the brain unit out of that engine tomorrow."

Alan looked out the viewport. He watched the space jockeys work on the *Valiant*'s one good engine. Fred and several others stood beside him. They were unable to work when they knew so much depended on what would happen next.

The engines were in long cones that stretched out from the rear of the ship. The jockeys were much smaller than the engine they were working on.

First they opened a panel at the very front of the cone. Then they carefully disconnected the brain unit.

Alan held his breath as the last bolt was freed. The jockeys lifted the unit out of the opening.

The brain unit was a metal cube about three feet long on each side. It was decorated with lights, gauges, and transport handles. It appeared to be intact, but none of the lights were lit.

The jockeys each grabbed a handle and pushed off. They glided smoothly toward the closest air lock. Alan and the others gathered at the doors. Before long the jockeys had come through the air lock. They placed the cube on the floor. Kay and Terry began their examination.

Alan watched nervously while the engineers worked. In the past few hours an inspection had been done on the engine itself. It seemed to be sound. As long as the brain unit was okay, the engine could be ignited. Then they could all go home. Every time Kay frowned, Alan felt butterflies in his stomach.

Terry announced the bad news.

"It's ruined," she said, holding up a thick purple crystal as long as her hand. She turned it for everyone to see the spider-web cracks across its surface. "The gem must have overloaded somehow when the missiles struck."

"How bad is it?" Fred asked.

Terry frowned. "Without the gem the brain won't accept commands. It's turned itself off."

"Don't we have replacement gems?" a midshipman asked.

"We did," said Terry. "They were kept in a cabinet that was vaporized during the battle."

"What about the other engines?" Fred asked. "Couldn't we borrow the gem from one of their brain units?"

"We should check, of course," Kay said. "But if this one overloaded, we can be pretty sure the others did, too."

"Can we bypass the gem?"

"I've heard of that being tried, but I don't know how to do it. The Avellar gem regulates the antimatter flow through the engine. If we go around it we could easily pump too much juice into the engine. It would explode. I doubt if even the chief engineer knows enough to attempt it."

Fred turned to Alan. "How is Ben?"

"Critical. But I expect him to live."

"We'll question him when he comes around," Fred stated.

The gems in the other brain units proved to be completely shattered. Alan strode through a quiet sick bay. He tried to shrug off the feeling of doom that had settled on the *Valiant*. The eyes of several patients followed him across the room. Everyone was waiting for word from him on the chief engineer's condition. Alan's report had remained the same for the past 24 hours. The patient was still unconscious.

Ben was in a tiny intensive-care room. When Alan entered, he found that the chief engineer had opened his eyes.

"Hi, Sport," Alan said. He tried to sound cheerful.

"Hi, Doc. How am I doing?" Ben's voice was strained but clear. His eyes were bright and alert. Alan decided it would be best to be direct.

"You're pretty torn up. But you're past the dangerous part. You won't be getting up for a while."

"What happened to the gravity?" Ben asked. "Is the ship that bad?"

Alan told him. Ben's frown grew deeper with each sentence. Finally Alan mentioned the Avellar crystal.

"I'm sorry," the chief said. "There's no way we could rig up a bypass. It would be suicide to try it."

Alan nodded, sighing. He made small talk as he checked Ben's progress. He kept his thoughts private. Ben did likewise. By the time Alan was through, Ben had fallen back to sleep.

Worried faces greeted Alan as soon as he left Ben's room. Alan paused.

"Ben says he might be able to do it. We'll have to wait until he's well enough to supervise."

Relief lit everyone's faces. Alan continued walking, hiding his own distress. In a few days, they'd find out he had lied. In the meantime, they would have hope. At the moment, hope was all that was keeping the *Valiant* together.

How was it that the Helvans put it? "The lie that gives hope is not a lie." It was one of the few Helvan sayings that Alan had memorized.

Alan, however, had no one to tell him comforting lies. He wondered, too, about the real value of what he'd done.

Alan stared out the viewport at the stars and dust clouds. The ship was so far out on the edge of the galaxy that no familiar suns could be seen. Alan came here when he needed to be someplace quiet. He was lost in thought and had barely noticed that Sheila had joined him.

Sheila said, "I thought I'd find you here, Doc."

"Really? Why?"

"You've been very quiet all day, ever since you saw Ben."

"I thought I was putting on a pretty good act," Alan said.

"I know your tricks, friend. Something's bothering you."

"Yes. I suppose it is." Alan made room for Sheila beside him. She sat down and gazed out the viewport.

"To be frank," Alan continued, "I was wondering what Helvan prison asteroids are like."

Sheila turned pale. She didn't need to hear what Ben had said. She knew now that the ship was sinking.

"How old are you, Sheila?"

"Twenty-eight."

Alan was ten years older. Both of them were far too young for their lives to end. He doubted they would be killed, but if they were taken by the Helvans it might seem like the same thing. The war had gone on for 20 years now; it might continue for 40 more.

"Maybe the Helvans need doctors," Alan said quietly. Even if he only got to treat other prisoners, that would be something.

"Look!" Sheila pointed out the viewport. Some of the stars were moving. They were getting larger. In a moment, the truth dawned on both of them.

"A spacecraft!" Alan blurted. Those weren't stars; they were running lights. One of them was blinking.

"Red alert! Red alert!" The sudden voice over the intercom made them jump. It was Fred's. "Battle stations!"

Alan and Sheila stood up and took a step toward sick bay. But Alan paused. Sheila bumped into him.

"Wait a minute," Alan said. "Why is a Helvan ship coming so close that we can see it?" He turned around. "Look. There's no exhaust glow. They're coasting in without power." As he watched, he began to notice a pattern to the blinking lights.

"They're signaling," Alan murmured. "That's Galactic Standard Code." He began to translate the light pulses into letters, then words.

"Gunnery ready for your order," said Zack's voice over the intercom.

Alan leaped for a nearby microphone and opened a channel. "Hold your fire!"

After a tense moment of silence, Fred spoke. "Alan? Was that you? What's going on?"

"Don't shoot!" Alan cried. *"They're doctors!"*

The ship **had** come close enough to reveal its shape. It was a lifeboat. Alan had recognized the signal being transmitted as the Helvan Doctor's Pledge: "Heal the body. Heal the mind. Heal the spirit."

The crew gathered in a restored rec room. Two very nervous Helvans, a man and a woman, stood in the center of the room. As more and more people crowded in, the aliens' light green faces turned almost white. It was easy to see how worried they were.

They were the only survivors of the ship the *Valiant* had fought. The lifeboat had been badly damaged in the attack. It would not hold air. The Helvans had crossed space wearing suits that soon would also have run out of air. It was silly to think the boat was a threat. Even its engine was out of order. The Helvans had reached the *Valiant* using only their steering jets.

Alan came forward and greeted the two in Helvan. His command of the language was weak, but he knew it better than any other *Valiant* crew member. The Helvans, both doctors, understood no English. That was why they had used the medical saying. It was the closest thing to a universal statement they knew.

As Alan spoke, he hoped his smile would convey his meaning. The Helvans stared in confusion.

Alan repeated himself. He held out the object in his hands. He was heady with the joy he felt over Terry's discovery. At the back of the Helvan lifeboat, she had found an intact Avellar gem.

"It's the same as ours!" she cried. "The size of the engine doesn't matter. It'll work in our stardrive."

Soon Alan made himself understood. The Helvans burst into smiles.

On this battleship, at least, the war had ended.